Diggers
and Cranes

Written by
Sally Hewitt and Nicola Wright

Designed by
Chris Leishman

Illustrated by
Rachael O'Neill

Contents

Backhoe loader 2

Excavators 4

Giant excavators 6

On the farm 8

Road building 10

Mining 12

Tunnelling 14

Tower cranes 16

Travelling cranes 18

Cranes in factories 20

Floating cranes 22

Index 24

CLB

Colour Library Books

Backhoe loader

The backhoe loader is two machines in one. It does some jobs with the hoe at the back and other jobs with the loader at the front.

There are windows all round so the driver can see in every direction.

Rams are pushed in and out to move the bucket back and forth.

Rams

Lugs on the wheels grip the ground.

Special features

The loader bucket has strong metal teeth for digging.

The bucket can also split in half to grab piles of soil.

The backhoe arm can lift up and down, reach out and pull in.

Bucket

The driver's seat can turn round to face the front or the back.

Arm

Backhoe

Stabilizers keep the machine steady while it is digging.

3

Excavators

Excavators are digging machines. Each of these excavators does a special sort of digging job.

Backhoe

Split bucket

Hammer

Hammermaster
The hammermaster has a powerful hammer to break up rocks and concrete.

Crawler tracks

Blade

Bulldozer
A bulldozer uses a heavy metal blade to clear the ground of rocks.

Split bucket

A split bucket opens and shuts like a mouth to bite into the earth.

Shovel

This special backhoe can swivel round to dig at the back, front or on either side.

Mini excavators and mini loaders are specially made to work in small spaces.

Mini skiploader

Mini excavator

with bucket and crawler tracks

Giant excavators

Rocks and stones used for building are
dug out of quarries. The biggest
excavators of all do this work.
They are called dragline excavators.

A dragline bucket is so big that a car could drive into it!

The enormous bucket scoops up huge amounts of rock.

Draglines are the wires that drag the bucket along the ground so that it fills up with rocks.

Some excavators can walk backwards and forwards on big metal pieces called shoes.

Quarrying cuts huge holes in the earth. Dragline excavators can also be used to fill the holes in again!

7

On the farm

Tractors with powerful engines and big wheels are very useful on farms. They can pull many different kinds of farm machines. All these machines get the ground ready for sowing seeds.

Tractor

Plough
A plough has sharp blades called ploughshares. They dig into the soil and turn it over.

Ploughshares

Roller
A roller smooths the soil and makes the field level.

Harrow
A harrow has rows of metal discs that cut the soil up into small pieces.

Metal discs

Seed drill

This is used to plant seeds in fields.

Hopper

Spikes

Furrows →

First the drill makes lines, called furrows, in the soil.

Seeds pass out of the hopper, down the drills into the furrows.

Spikes pull soil over the seeds.

9

Road building

The ground has to be cleared and flattened before a new road can be built. All these machines work together to do the job.

Compactor
Compactors drive up and down flattening the ground.

Blade

Metal feet

Blade

Grader
Graders use a blade to smooth over the surface.

Wheels

Blades

Scraper
Scrapers scrape away small bumps.

Bulldozer
Bulldozers clear big obstacles out of the way.

The scraper blade is lowered to the ground. A trap door lifts as it collects a load. When full the load is pushed out from the back.

Compactors have heavy metal wheels covered in spikes called feet. They push down into the soil.

Graders have long blades. They spread out small stones in an even layer.

Mining

Mining machines dig tunnels and cut coal, or metals such as gold, from deep under the ground.

Roadheader
A roadheader has spiky blades so it can bore tunnels through rock and earth.

Rock falls onto these wheels. The wheels turn and carry the rock away from where the machine is cutting.

Coal face cutter

This coal face cutter moves along the tunnel, cutting off coal from the wall of the mine.

Coal face

Blades

Roof supports strengthen the roof and walls of the tunnel so they do not fall in.

A **conveyor belt** carries the coal out of the tunnel.

Water sprays out of the coal cutter to damp down the coal dust.

Tunnelling

This giant tunnel-boring machine is called a TBM. TBMs were used to cut through rock to build the Channel Tunnel under the sea between England and France.

Metal plates grip the inside of the tunnel

A conveyor belt carries the dug-out earth out.

Rams push the cutting head forwards.

Cutting head

Concrete segments cover the inside of the tunnel.

The TBM control cabin has television cameras and computers.

Cutting head

This works like a drill. **Rams** push it against the rock. A big electric **motor** turns it round.

The huge cutting head can cut 12 cm of new tunnel in one minute.

Flyer Fun Fact

Each TBM machine needs a team of 44 workers to make it work!

Tower cranes

Cranes lift heavy things. Tower cranes work on building sites. They can lift heavy loads up to the top of the tallest buildings.

Hoist ropes lift and lower the hook and its load.

The lifting arm is called a jib. It can swivel round in a circle.

A trolley moves backwards and forwards along the jib, carrying the load.

A goose-neck crane has a jib that bends in the middle.

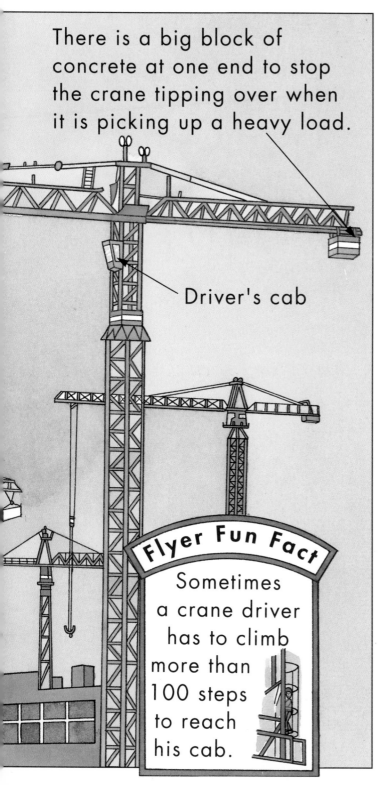

There is a big block of concrete at one end to stop the crane tipping over when it is picking up a heavy load.

Driver's cab

Flyer Fun Fact

Sometimes a crane driver has to climb more than 100 steps to reach his cab.

Hoists

Hoists are used for lifting.

A **beam hoist** can lift a window frame into place.

This hoist carries people and materials in a cage to the top of a tall building.

Access platforms lift workers into the air in a safety cage.

Travelling cranes

Some cranes are mounted on trucks or crawler tracks. This means they can travel from one place to another.

Truck crane

Heavy truck cranes have several sets of big wheels to carry their weight.

The boom opens up like a telescope.

Truck

Truck cab

Hook

Wheels

Outriggers are strong metal legs. They lift the wheels off the ground and hold the crane firmly in place.

Crawler tracks

Truck cranes can lift loads as heavy as 30 elephants!

Crawler crane

Crawler cranes can lift heavy loads and move along at the same time.

Crane cab

Crane controls

Hand levers and foot pedals are used to do these things:

Lift and lower the boom and the hook.

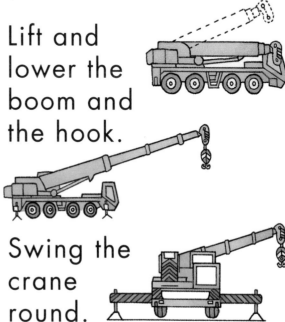

Swing the crane round.

The crane operator can see all round through the windows.

Cranes in factories

Travelling cranes are used in some factories. They are fixed above the factory floor and move backwards, forwards and sideways along rails.

This crane can lift a whole railway carriage.

The manipulator on the end of this crane lifts machinery off a conveyor onto a trolley.

Special lifting jobs

This crane has been specially made to lift and carry a bucket of hot molten metal.

This crane lifts and carries metal by picking it up with a very strong magnet.

A frame with special lifting pads can pick up and carry a huge sheet of heavy glass.

Floating cranes

Floating crane vessels work at sea. This one is building an offshore oil rig. It has two booms that lift parts into place.

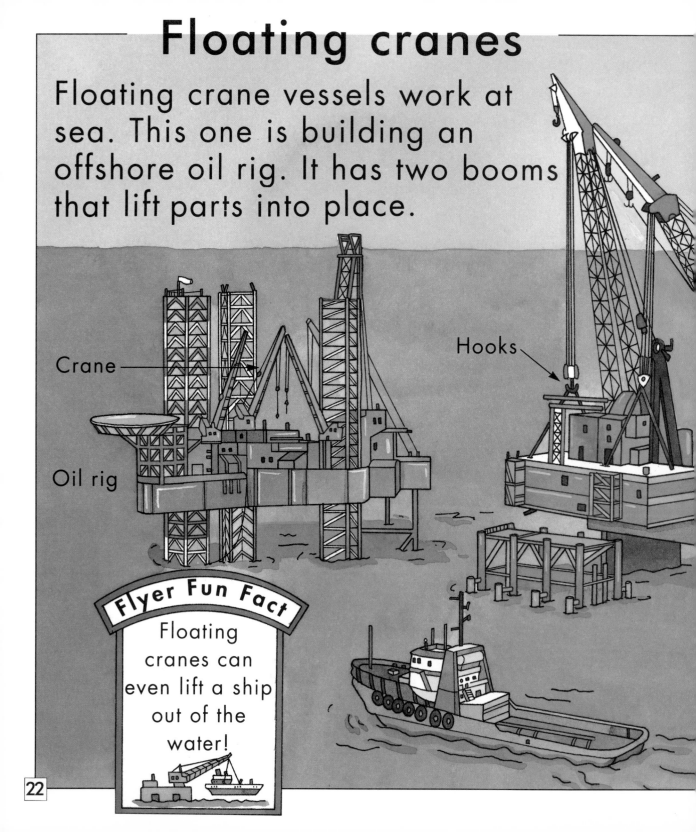

Hooks

Crane

Oil rig

Flyer Fun Fact

Floating cranes can even lift a ship out of the water!

About 350 people live and work on a floating crane vessel.

Helicopter

Boom

Helipad

Deck

There is a restaurant, cinema and hospital on board.

Huge **propellers** power the floating crane. It sails from one job to the next.

Helicopters carry workers and supplies to the oil rig and crane.

Smaller **floating cranes** are used to load and unload cargo ships when they are in harbour.

23

Index

Backhoe Loader 2-3
Bulldozer 4,10-11
Coal face cutter 13
Compactor 10-11
Cranes 16-17, 18-19, 20-21, 22-23
Crawler crane 19
Dragline excavator 6-7
Excavators 4-5, 6-7
Floating crane 22-23
Grader 11
Hammermaster 4
Harrow 9

Mini excavator 5
Mini skiploader 5
Plough 8
Roadheader 12
Roller 9
Scraper 11
Seed drill 9
Split bucket 5
TBM 14-15
Tower cranes 16-17
Tractor 8-9
Travelling cranes 20-21
Truck cranes 18

Edited by Nicola Wright & Dee Turner
Consultant: Andrew Woodward, B Eng
Series concept: Tony Potter
Design Manager: Kate Buxton
Colour separations by Scan Trans, Singapore
Printed by Proost, Belgium

This book was created by Zigzag Publishing Ltd, 5 High Street, Cuckfield, Sussex RH17 5EN

This edition published 1993 by Colour Library Books Ltd, Godalming, Surrey

CLB 3481
Copyright © Zigzag Publishing Ltd
ISBN 1 85833 090 4